I. Introduction

Is one better off being part of a small group, or a large one? In some contexts, there are clear advantages to being part of a small group. For example, it has been estimated that wages for individuals in smaller age cohorts earn more when entering the job market than those in larger cohorts (see, e.g., Welch, 1979). In other circumstances, there are advantages to being part of a large group. Some cases in which being part of a large group is advantageous include the outcome of voting and the purchase of products for which there is significant R&D required to create the product, such as pharmaceuticals and automobiles. With the graying of the baby boom generation, it is not surprising that products such as the prescription hair loss treatment Propecia and night-vision windshields for automobiles have reached the market.

In these two examples, the existence of a large market for a product appears to justify the high R&D expenses undertaken by the producer. This paper highlights a second, perhaps subtler advantage to being a member of a large group. Suppose a producer can develop information that shows his brand of a product works well for a specific "targeted" subset of the population (e.g., the effectiveness of his drug for a specific age group), but poorly for another group. Such "matching" information may not increase his unit sales, but can be profitable because it differentiates his brand, leading to higher prices.[1]

Previous work, such as Anderson and Renault (*A&R*, 2000) and Meurer and Stahl (*M&S*, 1994), has shown that information of this type can increase prices. Because information revelation leads to higher prices, which induce a transfer from consumers to producers, information may be

---

[1]In contrast, Grossman and Shapiro (1984) show that information about the existence and prices of rival goods results in greater substitutability between products, and lower prices.

1

privately profitable, but reduce welfare. M&S find that firms have an excess incentive to inform consumers of their product's characteristics, because firms' profits from providing information reflect gains due to both superior matches between consumers and products, and to the transfer from inframarginal consumers caused by the higher prices. A&R find that consumers overinvest in information about product characteristics because they ignore the transfer from other consumers to producers caused by the information. Hence, in both of these models, the private gain to information exceeds the social gain, and on the margin, too much information is produced.

This paper takes a somewhat different approach by assuming there are groups within the population (e.g., specific age groups) with common characteristics, and firms have information about the match between those characteristics and the features of their products. It analyzes the relationship between group size and the price effects of information.[2] Specifically, it shows that the marginal effect of information on price is increasing in the targeted group's size. It follows that even if the costs of gathering and revealing the information are proportional to the size of the group, the profitability of gathering and revealing the information will be increasing in group size, and hence information revelation may be profitable only for large targeted groups. In fact, this paper shows that the incentive to produce information may be less than socially optimal, especially for small groups.

These results might explain some apparent biases in drug research. It is often claimed that certain smaller groups of patients with a given ailment are underrepresented in clinical trials (e.g., female cardiac patients). Of course, one reason that male cardiac patients might receive more clinical attention is that there are economies of scale in clinical research (e.g., the size of the sample

---

[2]Whether it is appropriate to think of exogenous groups as existing in the population depends on the context. For pharmaceuticals, it seems appropriate to think of exogenously-determined groups (e.g., adult males) with a common "quality" parameter.

group required for obtaining FDA approval to list an additional indication or patient population for a drug is independent of the size of the user population). However, a second reason is suggested by this analysis; information about the suitability of a drug for male patients has a more-than-proportionally larger effect on price than information about female patients.

Explicitly modeling the role of group size permits analysis of another issue relating to the profitability of information revelation. An assumption made in the previous literature is that information is symmetric; that is, when information revelation increases the willingness to pay for a group who learn the brand is well-suited to them, there is another group of *the same size* whose willingness to pay falls. There are, however, circumstances in which information can have an asymmetric effect, whereby the size of the group whose willingness to pay increases is different from that of the group for whom it falls as a result. For example, suppose clinical trials have revealed that drugs A and B are equally effective in treating some ailment for the population as a whole. These clinical trials may conceal important differences in efficacy across groups within the population. That is, the producer of drug A may know from its clinical studies that its brand has greater efficacy for some subpopulation (e.g., cardiac patients who are also diabetics), which I refer to as the "targeted" group. If the average efficacy of the drug is fixed, this means that it is correspondingly less effective for some or all of the remaining population.[3] It need not be the case that the group for whom drug A's effectiveness is lower than average is the same size as the targeted group. For example, it could be that the subpopulation for whom the drug is more effective than its overall mean represents 20% of the population, while the drug is less effective than average for the entire

---

[3]In section V, I discuss the alternative interpretation that the information about the efficacy of drug for one group has no effect on the expected efficacy by patients in other groups.

remaining 80%.

Whether the information changes the perceived attributes of the product in a symmetric or asymmetric way has an impact on the price effects of the information, and consequently, on the profitability of releasing the information. In particular, information that increases a small group's willingness to pay for a product and simultaneously reduces it for a large group (holding the average willingness fixed) can *lower* the equilibrium profit from selling that product. The reason is that the firm's total sales decline because the increased sales from a large increase in willingness to pay for a small group is less than sales loss from a small decrease in it for a large group. In contrast, if the group for which willingness to pay falls is the same size (or smaller) than the group for which it rises, the firm's profits will rise.

II. The effect of information on prices

In evaluating the effect of information on prices and output, and the consequent incentive to disseminate information about product characteristics, I consider a simple duopoly model, along the lines developed by A&R and M&S. As in those models, information is truthful, and known to be truthful by all consumers. Consumers buy at most one unit of a product, two differentiated brands of which are available from two competing sellers. As in the previous work, I normalize the production costs to zero, although it is costly to inform consumers of each brand's characteristics.

I depart from this prior work by treating consumers as heterogeneous in two respects; one aspect that is observable to the sellers, which I refer to as the consumer's group (e.g., female and over 65 years of age), and one aspect that is idiosyncratic and unobservable. Specifically, in each of the K groups, all consumers in that group have a common parameter representing their valuation

4

of brand i (i = A, B) relative to an outside option, and in addition, each consumer has an idiosyncratic valuation for each product. Hence, for consumer j in group k, the utility from brand i relative to the outside option (and hence, j's reservation value) is $U_j = \alpha_i^k - P_i + \epsilon_{ij}$, where α_i^k is the value of systematic component of brand i's "quality" to all consumers in group k, and ϵ_{ij} is consumer j's idiosyncratic valuation of brand i. I assume that ϵ_{ij} is I.I.D. for the two brands for any group, and ϵ_{ij} is distributed identically for all groups, with support $(0, \bar{e})$ for both brands. For concreteness, one can think of α_i^k as the average success rate of drug i in treating an ailment for patients in group k, multiplied by each consumer's value of a successful treatment, and ϵ_{ij} as consumer j's (unobservable) idiosyncratic valuation of the drug.[4] Quality is unambiguously defined for each consumer (in that utility is increasing in α_i, all else equal), but the valuation of the brand varies across consumers within each group (in this sense, brands are horizontally differentiated). Consumer j (who is a member of group k) prefers brand A to brand B if $\alpha_A^k - P_A + \epsilon_{Aj} > \alpha_B^k - P_B + \epsilon_{Bj}$. This condition can usefully be written $R = \epsilon_{Aj} - \epsilon_{Bj} > \alpha_B^k - \alpha_A^k + P_A - P_B$. The absence of superscripts on P_A and P_B reflects the assumption that firms cannot price discriminate, but instead charge the same price to all groups. Firm A's share of sales to group k is

$$S_A^k = \int_{\alpha_B^k - \alpha_A^k + P_A - P_B}^{\bar{e}} df(R)dR$$

---

[4] In the drug example, *product* corresponds to a class of drugs (e.g., H_2 antagonists for ulcers) and *brand* corresponds to a specific chemical (e.g., Tagamet or Zantac). Note that specific differences in the relative efficacy of drugs within a class for different individuals can sometimes be dramatic. For example, while the two leading anti-herpetics are roughly equally effective for most patients, only one is approved for use in immuno-compromised (e.g., HIV positive) individuals. One example of ϵ_{ij} is consumer j's valuation of the side effects of drug i. In this case, the support of ϵ_{ij} might be most appropriately thought as $(-\bar{e}, 0)$. However, the analysis in the paper can be generalized to negative ϵ_{ij} with appropriate reinterpretation of the α_i^k.

as long as $|\alpha_B^k - \alpha_A^k + P_A - P_B| < \bar{e}$. If this inequality does not hold for some k, we refer to α_A^k as a *drastic* difference in quality.[5] If the quality difference is drastic for some k, then $S_A^k = 0$ or 1, depending on the sign of $\alpha_B^k - \alpha_A^k$ for any particular k. Information will tend to be drastic when consumer heterogeneity within groups is small relative to differences across groups. Normalizing the number of consumers to 1, the aggregate demand for A's product is S_A^k summed across groups,

$$Q_A = \sum_{k=1}^{K} w_k \, S_A^k \quad (1)$$

where w_k is the percentage of the population in group k. The assumptions regarding ϵ_{ij} imply that for every group, R has support $(-\bar{e}, \bar{e})$. I also assume that R is symmetrically distributed around 0, with $f(\bar{e}) = f(-\bar{e}) = 0$, and $f'(R) < 0$ for $R > 0$, $f'(R) > 0$ for $R < 0$, $f'(0) = 0$ (i.e., F(R) is unimodal).[6]

As in A&R and M&S, I assume the two brands are on average, equally attractive. Here, this means that $\Sigma \, w_k \, \alpha_A^k = \Sigma \, w_k \, \alpha_B^k = \hat{\alpha}$. Returning to the drug example, $\hat{\alpha}$ can be interpreted as the monetary value of a successful treatment multiplied by the average efficacy of the two drugs in curing patients with some ailment for the population as a whole. In the absence of information, consumers in all groups view $\hat{\alpha}$ as the appropriate estimate of this value (that is, $\alpha_i^k = \hat{\alpha}$ for all k, i = A, B). Firms may have the ability to change these estimates of α_A^k for some groups. In the drug example, firms may have information from clinical trials that allows them to better match patients to drugs. For example, the manufacturer of drug A may know that it has a higher success rate among

---

[5]This use of the term *drastic* parallels the use in the R&D literature (see, e.g., Reinganum, 1988). In the R&D literature, drastic refers to a cost reduction due to innovation that is sufficiently large that the old technology is not a binding constraint on the seller of the innovation. Analogously, here drastic refers to information that leads to the rival brand no longer serving as a constraint when selling to the targeted group.

[6]The condition that $f(\bar{e}) = f(-\bar{e}) = 0$ implies that demand is continuously differentiable.

women than among men. In terms of the model, information consists of a set of $\alpha_A^{\ k}$ that can differ across groups, even though there is still heterogeneity within groups. In contrast, in both the A&R and M&S models, $U_j = \epsilon_{ij} - P_i$, and $\alphâ$ is the expected value of ϵ_{ij}.[7] In these models, information consists of consumers learning their ϵ_{ij}, and consequently learning which brand better suits them. As in the previous work, here information about the $\alpha_A^{\ k}$ has effects on prices. Because demand is continuously differentiable, we can take the derivative of Q_A with respect to P_A which is $-\Sigma\ w_k\ f(\alpha_B - \alpha_A + P_A - P_B) < 0$ (note that $f(\ )$ is zero if the information is drastic for some group), so that firm A's first-order condition with respect to its price is

$$\sum_k w_k\ S_A^k - P_A \sum_k w_k\ f(P_A - P_B + \alpha_B^k - \alpha_A^k) = 0 \quad (2)$$

and B's first-order condition is

$$\sum_k w_k\ S_B^k - P_B \sum_k w_k\ f(P_B - P_A + \alpha_A^k - \alpha_B^k) = 0 \quad (3)$$

These conditions imply that the slopes of the two firms' best response functions are

$$\frac{\partial P_A * (P_B)}{\partial P_B} = \frac{\sum_k w_k\ f(P_A - P_B + \alpha_B^k - \alpha_A^k) + P_A \sum_k w_k\ f'(P_A - P_B + \alpha_B^k - \alpha_A^k)}{2\sum_k w_k\ f(P_A - P_B + \alpha_B^k - \alpha_A^k) + P_A \sum_k w_k\ f'(P_A - P_B + \alpha_B^k - \alpha_A^k)} \quad (4)$$

$$\frac{\partial P_B * (P_A)}{\partial P_A} = \frac{\sum_k w_k\ f(P_B - P_A + \alpha_A^k - \alpha_B^k) + P_B \sum_k w_k\ f'(P_B - P_A + \alpha_A^k - \alpha_B^k)}{2\sum_k w_k\ f(P_B - P_A + \alpha_A^k - \alpha_B^k) + P_B \sum_k w_k\ f'(P_B - P_A + \alpha_A^k - \alpha_B^k)} \quad (5)$$

Because the average quality, $\alphâ$, is assumed fixed, the information that $\alpha_A^{\ L} > \alphâ$ implies that $\alpha_A^{\ k} < \alphâ$ for one or more other groups.[8] For any given $\alpha_A^{\ L} > \alphâ$, there are multiple ways that the other

---

[7]In M&S, $\epsilon_{ij} = V$ for one product, and zero for the other, while the ϵ_{ij} are I.I.D. in the A&R model.

[8]In section V, I consider a different interpretation of information, where the average efficacy changes with the information. Specifically, section V considers what happens if $\alpha_A^{\ k}$

$\alpha_A{}^k$ can change so that the average quality remains $\hat{\alpha}$. As shown below, how the other $\alpha_A{}^k$ change with the information about $\alpha_A{}^L$ will affect the resultant price effect of any given $\alpha_A{}^L > \hat{\alpha}$. In this section, I consider "symmetric" changes in the $\alpha_A{}^k$. The following section analyzes "asymmetric" changes.

Definition: A distribution of the $\alpha_A{}^k$ is symmetric if whenever $\alpha_A{}^L > \hat{\alpha}$ for some group of size w_L then there is some other group of size $w_M = w_L$ for which $\alpha_A{}^M$ is less than $\hat{\alpha}$ by the same amount.

An implication of a symmetric distribution of the $\alpha_A{}^k$ is that $\alpha_A{}^M + \alpha_A{}^L = 2\hat{\alpha}$. For example, if group L consists of individuals under 20 years of age (who comprise 30% of the relevant population) and has $\alpha_A{}^L > \hat{\alpha}$, then the distribution of the $\alpha_A{}^k$ will be symmetric if the group for which $\alpha_A{}^M < \hat{\alpha}$ also represents 30% of the population, but will be asymmetric if the group for which $\alpha_A{}^M < \hat{\alpha}$ includes all individuals 20 and over.

When information is symmetric, a pure strategy symmetric equilibrium in prices can emerge. Specifically, letting $P^S = P_A{}^S = P_B{}^S$, if

$$w_L(\alpha_A^1 - \hat{\alpha}_B - \bar{e}) < P^S/2 \qquad (6)$$

then, as shown below, there exists a pure strategy symmetric pricing equilibrium. In words, inequality (6) says that the maximum profit firm A can earn by selling to group L only is less than its profits at the symmetric equilibrium. Rewriting (6) as

$$\alpha_A{}^L - \hat{\alpha} - \bar{e} < (1-w_L)P^S/(2\, w_L) \qquad (6'),$$

two observations following directly

Observation 1: The left-hand side of (6') is < 0 for non-drastic $\alpha_A{}^L$, and ≥ 0 for drastic $\alpha_A{}^L$. Hence

———————————————

remains equal to $\hat{\alpha}$ for other groups, while $\alpha_A{}^1 > \hat{\alpha}$.

for any positive P^S, (6) holds for all non-drastic α_A^L, and some drastic α_A^L.

Observation 2: If $\partial P^S/\partial \alpha_A^L < (1-w_1)/(2\ w_1)$, then (6) will fail to hold for α_A^L sufficiently large.

In what follows, I focus on the pure strategy equilibrium that emerges when (6) holds. Note that when (6) does not hold, then the only equilibria feature mixed strategies.

Proposition 1: Holding $\alpha_B^k = \hat{\alpha}$ for all k, an equilibrium exists with $P_A = P_B$ for symmetric distributions of the α_A^k if condition (6) holds

Proof: Let $\alpha_A^1 > \hat{\alpha}$ and $\alpha_A^2 < \hat{\alpha}$ such that $\hat{\alpha} - \alpha_A^2 = \alpha_A^1 - \hat{\alpha}$ and $w_1 = w_2$. First suppose α_A^1 is not drastic. This implies that at $P_A = P_B$,

$$Q_A = \frac{1 - 2\ w_1}{2} + w_1 \int_{\hat{\alpha}_B - \alpha_A^1}^{\bar{e}} df(R)\ dR + w_2 \int_{\alpha_A^1 - \hat{\alpha}_B}^{\bar{e}} df(R)\ dR$$

which is equal to ½ by virtue of the symmetry of f(R). Similarly $Q_B = ½$. Substituting into (2) and (3) yields

and
$$P_A^S = \frac{1}{2[w_1\ f(\hat{\alpha}_B - \alpha_A^1) + w_2\ f(\alpha_A^1 - \hat{\alpha}_B) + (1 - 2\ w_1)f(0)]} \qquad (7)$$

$$P_B^S = \frac{1}{2[w_1\ f(\alpha_A^1 - \hat{\alpha}_B) + w_2\ f(\hat{\alpha}_B - \alpha_A^1) + (1 - 2\ w_1)f(0)]} \qquad (8)$$

Because of the symmetry of F(R), $f(\hat{\alpha}_B - \alpha_A^1) = f(\alpha_A^1 - \hat{\alpha}_B)$ and since $w_1 = w_2$, both first-order conditions are met at the price which solves equation (7) (or equivalently, (8)).

If the information is drastic, the demand facing retailer A is $Q_A = w_1 + (1 - w_1 - w_2)\ S_A$ (as long as $P_A < \alpha_A^1 - \hat{\alpha} - \bar{e} + P_B$) while B's demand is $Q_B = w_2 + (1 - w_1 - w_2)\ S_B$ (assuming $P_B < -\alpha_A^1 + \hat{\alpha} - \bar{e} + P_A$). Since $w_1 = w_2$, solving equations (2) and (3) yields

9

$$P_A^s = P_B^s = \frac{1}{2(1 - 2\ w_1)f(0)} \quad (9)$$

Note that $P_A < \alpha_A^1 - \bar{\alpha} - \bar{e} + P_B$ and $P_B < \bar{\alpha} - \alpha_A^1 - \bar{e} + P_A$, at $P_A^S = P_B^S$. In addition, as long as w_1 $(\alpha_A^1$

$- \bar{\alpha} - \bar{e}) < P_A^S/2$, firm A's profits at P_A^S exceed the profits that he could earn by selling to group 1

only. Hence, as long as condition (6) is satisfied, $P^S = 1/[2*(1-2\ w_1)\ f(0)]$ maximizes each firm's

profits.

Finally, because $w_1\ f'(R) = -\ w_2\ f'(-R)$ and $f'(R) = 0$ for all other groups, whether the

information is drastic or non-drastic, the best response functions have slopes of ½ at P^S, and $P_A^S =$

P_B^S represents an equilibrium. ∎

This lemma establishes the existence of a symmetric pricing equilibrium for symmetric

distributions of the α_A^ks for which condition (6) holds. The prices in these symmetric equilibria

depend on two parameters; $\alpha_A^1 - \bar{\alpha}$, and w_1, and it useful to write the prices as function of those

parameters; i.e., $P_A^S(\alpha_A^1, w_1)$. Figure 1 portrays for relationship between $P_A^S(\alpha_A^1, w_1)$ and α_A^1 for

$\alpha_A^1 - \bar{\alpha} < 7$. As can be seen there, prices are lowest in the absence of information. In the absence

of information, $\alpha_A^k = \bar{\alpha}$ for all groups and equations (7) and (8) imply that $P_A^S = 1/(2\ f(0))$. Since

$f(\alpha_A^1 - \bar{\alpha})$ is less than $f(0)$, this means that the prices are higher than $1/(2\ f(0))$ whenever there is non-

drastic information. Equations (7) - (8) imply that the symmetric equilibrium price is increasing in

α_A^1 for non-drastic α_A^1. Comparing equations (7) and (8) with equation (9), we see that in the limit

as $\alpha_A^1 - \bar{\alpha}$ approaches $\bar{e}$ (the information approaches being drastic), the prices determined by

equations (7) and (8) approach the price in equation (9). Finally, while equation (9) implies that

prices are higher than $1/(2\ f(0))$ whenever there is drastic information, it also implies that $\partial P^S / \partial \alpha_A^1$

$= 0$; once the information is drastic. Returning to Observations (1) and (2), this last fact implies that equation (6) will be satisfied for some drastic α_A^1, but it may be profitable for firm A to deviate if α_A^1 is drastic and sufficiently large.

One way of thinking about the effect of symmetric targeted information is that an increase in the perceived value of a brand for one group (accompanied by lower value for an identical-sized group) reduces the impact of a higher price on unit sales (because the density function is lower when evaluated at higher values of $|\alpha_A^k - \alpha_B^k|$), without changing the level of sales. Such a change increases the profit-maximizing price and the revenues of the firm revealing the information. In the following section, I show that asymmetric changes in the α_A^k can have a different effect because they can influence both the responsiveness of customers to price changes and total sales. For this reason, the revelation of information about the α_A^k can have ambiguous effects on A's price and revenues.

One other observation follows directly from equations (7) - (9); prices are increasing in w_1. Hence, while firm A's market share is ½ in all symmetric equilibria, its profits (gross of the cost of informing consumers) are increasing in the targeted group's size. In fact, even if it is costly to gather and disseminate the information and those costs are proportional to group size, the profits from informing consumers about a given α_A^1 are increasing in the targeted group's size, as shown below.[9]

Proposition 2: Assume condition (6) holds and suppose the costs of gathering and disseminating information are proportional to the size of the group - i.e., information costs are $\gamma\, w_1$ (where $\gamma > 0$). If it is profitable to inform a group of size $\tilde{w}_1$ about a particular $\alpha_A^1 > \hat{\alpha}$, then

---

[9]Information costs are here modeled as if firm A knew α_A^1 and was calculating the profitability of publicizing that information. A more realistic interpretation (which is analytically similar) is that information costs include the manufacturer's cost of conducting the R&D to determine α_A^1 (multiplied by the probability he finds $\alpha_A^1 > \hat{\alpha}$) plus the costs of publicizing that information.

1. it will be profitable to inform a group of size $w_1 \in (\tilde{w}_1, \frac{1}{2}.)$ (i.e., a larger group) about that α_A^1.

2. it may be unprofitable to inform a group of size $w_1 \in (0, \tilde{w}_1)$.

Proof: Suppose there is some $\tilde{w}_1 \in (0, \frac{1}{2})$ such that for α_A^1, $Q_A P_A^S(\alpha_A^1, \tilde{w}_1) - Q_A P_A^S(\hat{\alpha}) - \gamma \tilde{w}_1/2 = \theta/2 > 0$; that is, at $\tilde{w}_1$, releasing the information about α_A^1 increases revenues by $\theta/2$ more than it does costs. I wish to demonstrate that for any larger group, $\delta\tilde{w}_1$ (where $\delta > 1$, $\delta \tilde{w}_1 < \frac{1}{2}$), releasing the information is strictly profitable, while releasing the information will be unprofitable for a group smaller than $\tilde{w}_1$ for θ sufficiently small. For a group other than $\tilde{w}_1$ in size, the change in profits from releasing the information is $Q_A P_A^S(\alpha_A^1, \delta \tilde{w}_1) - Q_A P_A^S(\hat{\alpha}) - \delta\gamma \tilde{w}_1/2$ which is equal to $Q_A P_A^S(\alpha_A^1, \delta\tilde{w}_1) - Q_A P_A^S(\hat{\alpha}) - \delta[Q_A P_A^S(\alpha_A^1, \tilde{w}_1) - Q_A P_A^S(\hat{\alpha}) - \theta/2]$. To evaluate the sign of this expression, first consider the case of drastic information. If condition (6) holds, and the information is drastic, then $Q_A = \frac{1}{2}$, and $Q_A P_A^S(\alpha_A^1, \delta \tilde{w}_1) - Q_A P_A^S(\hat{\alpha}_A) - \delta[Q_A P_A^S(\alpha_A^1, \tilde{w}_1) - Q_A P_A^S(\hat{\alpha}) - \theta/2]$ equals

$$\frac{1}{4}\left[\frac{1}{(1 - 2\delta\tilde{w}_1)f(0)} - \frac{1}{f(0)} - \frac{\delta}{(1 - 2 \tilde{w}_1)f(0)} + \frac{\delta}{f(0)}\right] + \frac{\delta\theta}{2}$$

$$= \frac{1}{4f(0)}\left[\frac{1}{1 - 2\delta\tilde{w}_1} - \frac{\delta}{(1 - 2\tilde{w}_1)} + \delta - 1\right] + \frac{\delta\theta}{2} = \frac{1}{4(1 - 2\delta\tilde{w}_1)f(0)}\left[1 - \delta\left(\frac{1 - 2\delta\tilde{w}_1}{1 - 2\tilde{w}_1}\right) + (\delta - 1)(1 - 2\delta\tilde{w}_1)\right] + \frac{\delta\theta}{2}$$

$$= \frac{(\delta - 1)4\tilde{w}_1^2\delta}{4f(0)(1 - 2\delta\tilde{w}_1)(1 - 2\tilde{w}_1)} + \frac{\delta\theta}{2} \quad (10)$$

since $2\delta \tilde{w}_1 < 1$, this is positive for $\delta > 1$. Hence, releasing the information is strictly profitable for all $w_1 \in (\tilde{w}_1, \frac{1}{2})$. Conversely, expression (10) will be negative for $\delta < 1$ and θ sufficiently small. Finally, when α_A^1 is not drastic, the analogue of expression (10) is

12

$$k(\delta-1)4\tilde{w}_1^2\delta[f(0) \; + \; (f(\hat{\alpha}-\alpha_A^1+P_A-P_B))^2 \; - \; 2f(\hat{\alpha}-\alpha_A^1+P_A-P_B)] + \frac{\delta\theta}{2} \qquad (10')$$

$$where \; k = \frac{\tilde{w}_1^2\delta f(\hat{\alpha}-\alpha_A^1+P_A-P_B)}{[2\delta\tilde{w}_1 \; f(\hat{\alpha}-\alpha_A^1+P_A-P_B)+(1-2\delta\tilde{w}_1)f(0)][2\tilde{w}_1 \; f(\hat{\alpha}-\alpha_A^1+P_A-P_B)+(1-2\tilde{w}_1)f(0)]} > 0$$

Since $f(0) + f(\alpha_A{}^1 - \hat{\alpha} + P_A - P_B) + - 2f(\alpha_A{}^1 - \hat{\alpha} + P_A - P_B) > 0$, this implies that, as was the case for

drastic information, (10') is positive for $\delta > 1$, and negative for $\delta < 1$ and θ sufficiently small. ∎

The implication of this result is that firms will have (weakly) less incentive to gather

information which benefits small groups, even if the cost of generating and disseminating that

information is proportional to the size of the group, and the average reservation value of the

members of all groups are the same.

Whether the per-individual costs of informing a group of consumers are increasing or

decreasing in group size depends on the specific context. For prescription drugs, information costs

are likely to increase less than proportionally with group size in most cases. For example, to

establish efficacy for a group, the FDA requires tests whose sample sizes are independent of the size

of the group. In addition, to the extent that informing physicians is the easiest way to disseminate

the information, economies of scale seem likely, since the number of relevant physicians may be

independent of group size.[10] This is consistent with the frequently-expressed concern that certain

smaller groups (e.g., female cardiac patients) are underrepresented in clinical studies.[11]

III. The Effects of Asymmetric Information

---

[10]For some drugs, there may be some specialization between physicians and patients (i.e., pediatricians), so that it may be fairly inexpensive to target the relevant group.

[11]Perhaps in recognition of this effect, the FDA offers incentives for drug companies   to perform clinical studies on children (who often represent a small share of patients).

Holding the average quality of a brand of a product fixed, information that reveals a superior match between that brand and consumers in a specific group necessarily reduces the suitability of that brand for some or all of the remaining population. In some circumstances, it is plausible that, contrary to the assumption of symmetry made in the previous section, this reduction in suitability occurs for a different-sized group than the group that experiences increased suitability.[12] As discussed in an earlier example, information that a drug is particularly suitable to patients under 20 years old could be interpreted as information that it is less suitable for all patients 20 and over.

This section explores the implications of such asymmetric information on prices and profits. I assume that the information has a positive effect on the suitability of a brand of a product for a targeted group representing less than one-half the population. I further assume that the cost of informing this group are the same whether the information is symmetric or asymmetric. Finally, I assume that the information has a negative effect on the remaining population that is uniform across all non-targeted groups.[13] That is, firm A's information is that α_A^1 is greater than $\hat{\alpha}$ and $\alpha_A^k = (\hat{\alpha} - w_1 \alpha_A^1)/(1-w_1) < \hat{\alpha}$ for all non-targeted groups, with $w_1 < \frac{1}{2}$ and α_A^k non-drastic (although α_A^1 may be drastic). Not surprisingly, such information increases sales to the targeted group, and reduces sales to the other groups. As Proposition 3 shows, the second effect dominates and total sales fall.

---

[12] A third possibility, which is discussed in section V, is that an increase in α_A^1 has no effect on the other α_A^k, in which case the information increases average quality.

[13] Of course, information could also be asymmetric if the group whose α_A fell comprises less than all of the remaining population. If the group whose α_A falls is actually smaller than the group for whom it rises, the analysis is similar, except that the effects on the two firms are reversed. That is, similar analysis to Proposition 3 shows that firm A's sales increase from revealing the information.

Proposition 3: Suppose $\alpha_A^1 > \hat{\alpha}_A$ and $\alpha_A^k = (\hat{\alpha}_A - w_1 \alpha_A^1)/(1-w_1)$, with $w_1 < \frac{1}{2}$. Then, evaluated at $P_A = P_B$, A's sales are decreasing in α_A^1.

Proof: For α_A^1 non-drastic, evaluated at $P_A = P_B$, $\partial Q_A/\partial \alpha_A^1 = w_1 [f(\hat{\alpha}_B - \alpha_A^1) - f((w_1(\alpha_A^1 - \hat{\alpha}_B)/(1-w_1))]$, since $\alpha_A^k = \hat{\alpha}_A - w_1 \alpha_A^1/(1-w_1)$ for $k > 1$. This is negative for $w_1 < \frac{1}{2}$, since $f(R)$ evaluated at $w_1(\alpha_A^1 - \hat{\alpha}_B)/(1-w_1)$ is greater than $f(R)$ evaluated at $\alpha_A^1 - \alpha_B^1$. For α_A^1 drastic, $\partial Q_A/\partial \alpha_A^1 = w_1[- f(w_1(\alpha_A^1 - \hat{\alpha}_B)/(1-w_1) + P_A - P_B] < 0$. ∎

That is, information that α_A^1 is greater than $\hat{\alpha}$ that is asymmetric lowers A's sales, other things equal. Of course, to determine the effect of the information on A's profits, one has to determine the effect on A's price. Making this determination requires additional structure in the model.[14] Specifically, I assume that the ϵ_{ij} are distributed uniformly with support $(0,1)$. This implies F is symmetric with support $(-1,1)$, and $f(R) = 1 + R$ for $R \leq 0$, and $f(R) = 1 - R$ for $R \geq 0$.

Under this assumption, the symmetric equilibrium prices with no targeted information are $P_A^s(\hat{\alpha}) = P_B^s(\hat{\alpha}) = 1/[2(f(0)] = \frac{1}{2}$, so that each firm's profits are $1/4$. If firm A releases non-drastic asymmetric information that the α_A^1 for the targeted group is greater than $\hat{\alpha}$, with $\alpha_A^k = (\hat{\alpha} - w_1 \alpha_A^1)/(1-w_1)$ for all other groups, the demand facing the two firms is

$$Q_A = \frac{1}{2} + \frac{(1-2w_1)(P_A - P_B)^2}{2} + (1 - 2w_1(\alpha_A^1 - \hat{\alpha}))(P_B - P_A) + \frac{w_1(\alpha_A^1 - \hat{\alpha})^2(2w_1 - 1)}{2(1-w_1)} \quad (11)$$

$$Q_B = \frac{1}{2} - \frac{(1-2w_1)(P_B - P_A)^2}{2} + (1 - 2w_1(\alpha_A^1 - \hat{\alpha}))(P_A - P_B) - \frac{w_1(\alpha_A^1 - \hat{\alpha})^2(2w_1 - 1)}{2(1-w_1)} \quad (12)$$

Given this distribution of R, one can also calculate the demand facing firm A if the

___

[14] Holding $\alpha_B^k = \hat{\alpha}$ for all k, $\partial P^*_B(P_A)/\partial \alpha_A^1 > 0$ if w_1 is less $\frac{1}{2}$. That is, the information shifts out B's best response function. However, the effect on $P^*_A(P_B)$ is ambiguous, so that the effect of information on prices is ambiguous. In fact, as Figure 5 below demonstrates, it is possible that information can lower P_A.

information is symmetric and non-drastic. It differs from (11) only by one term; the term involving

$(\alpha_A^1 - \hat{\alpha})^2$ is absent in the symmetric case. Since that term is negative (because $w_1 < \frac{1}{2}$), this means

that, other things equal, Q_A is lower in the asymmetric case (consistent with Proposition 2).

However, since $\partial Q_A / \partial P_A$ is the same in the two cases, we have

Lemma 1: For any given non-drastic $\alpha_A^1 > \hat{\alpha}$, firm A's profit-maximizing price will be higher if the

information is symmetric than asymmetric, when ϵ_{ij} is uniform on $(0,1)$.

Proof: Firm A's first-order condition with respect to its price in the asymmetric case equals

$$0 = \frac{1}{2} + \frac{(1 - 2w_1)(P_A - P_B)^2}{2} + (1 - 2w_1(\alpha_A^1 - \hat{\alpha}))(P_B - P_A) + \frac{w_1(\alpha_A^1 - \hat{\alpha})^2(2w_1 - 1)}{2(1 - w_1)} + P_A[(1 - 2w_1)(P_A - P_B) - (1 - 2w_1(\alpha_A^1 - \hat{\alpha}))] \quad (13)$$

Evaluated at $P_A = P_A^S(\alpha_A^1, w_1)$, $P_B = P_B^S(\alpha_A^1, w_1)$, this equals

$$0 = \frac{1}{2} + \frac{w_1(\alpha_A^1 - \hat{\alpha})^2(2w_1 - 1)}{2(1 - w_1)} - P_A[1 - 2w_1(\alpha_A^1 - \hat{\alpha})] \quad (13')$$

and since $P_A^S = 1/(2(1 - 2w_1(\alpha_A^1 - \hat{\alpha})))$, this equals $w_1(\alpha_A^1 - \hat{\alpha})^2(2w_1 - 1)/(2(1 - w_1))$ which is negative.

It follows that evaluated at $P_B = P_B^S(\alpha_A^1, w_1)$, firm A's profit-maximizing price is lower in the

asymmetric case. ∎

Similarly, the expression for Q_B in the symmetric, non-drastic case differs from equation (12)

by the last term only. In equation (12), the last term is positive, which implies that the Q_B will be

higher in the asymmetric case. As was the case for firm A, the slope of firm B's demand curve

does not change between the two cases. Hence,

Lemma 2: For any given non-drastic $\alpha_A^1 > \alpha_B^1$, firm B's profit-maximizing price will be lower if the

information is symmetric than asymmetric when ϵ_{ij} is uniform on $(0,1)$.

Proof: Follows same logic as Lemma 1.■

The intuition behind these lemmas is that compared to the symmetric case, asymmetric information increases B's sales and decreases A's sales, without changing the slope of either firm's demand curve. Hence, for firm A, the number of marginal customers is the same whether a given α_A^1 is symmetric or asymmetric, but the number of inframarginal consumers is lower in the asymmetric case, leading firm A to charge a lower price (and conversely for firm B). Hence, while the assumption that ϵ_{ij} is uniform on $(0,1)$ does not allow one to calculate equilibrium prices, it does allow one to determine how the best-response functions differ between symmetric and asymmetric cases. This in turn implies

Proposition 4: Compared to the symmetric equilibrium, P_A will be lower and P_B will be higher with asymmetric information for α_A^1 non-drastic, when ϵ_{ij} is uniform on $(0,1)$.

Proof: Compared to the symmetric equilibrium, A's best-response function is lower and B's is higher by equal amounts in the asymmetric equilibrium. This implies an increase in P_B and a decrease in P_A, since both best-response functions have slopes between 0 and 1. ■

Figures 2 and 3 shows how A's price and profits vary with the two parameters in the symmetric and asymmetric non-drastic cases. These results illustrate Proposition 4 - both A's prices and profits are higher in the symmetric case. Figure 2 shows the prices in the two cases as functions of w_1 for $\alpha_A^1 - \hat{\alpha} = .5$. Figure 3 indicates that, at this value of $\alpha_A^1 - \hat{\alpha}$, profits in both cases are increasing in w_1 and that A's profits are higher in the symmetric equlibrium. Although not depicted there, B's prices and profits are higher in the asymmetric case. Figure 4 shows the effect of higher $\alpha_A^1 - \hat{\alpha}$ on prices and profits (for $w_1 = .25$).

Unfortunately, the relationship between the asymmetric and symmetric reaction curves in the drastic case depends on the values of the two parameters. For example, when $\alpha_A^1 - \acute{\alpha} = 1$, prices and profits are higher for both firms in the symmetric equilibrium than in the asymmetric one for all values of w_1. In fact, for certain values of w_1, firm A's profits with drastic asymmetric information can actually be lower than in the initial, "no information" equilibrium. The reason is that drastic asymmetric information increases a small group's valuation of brand A by a large amount, while reducing a large group's value of it by a small amount. Since the density function is lower when evaluated at higher values of $|\alpha_A^k - \alpha_B^k|$, large changes in information have proportionately smaller effects on sales than small changes.[15] Hence, firm A's sales fall, and even though its (absolute) demand elasticity falls as well, the net effect on A's profits could be negative. Figure 5 shows the relationship between $\alpha_A^1 - \acute{\alpha}$ and firm A's prices and profits for $w_1 = .1$. Note that in both the asymmetric and symmetric equilibria, both prices and profits are increasing in α_A^1 for $\alpha_A^1 - \acute{\alpha}$ non-drastic (i.e., less than 1). However, for $\alpha_A^1 - \acute{\alpha} > 1$, A's profits in the asymmetric case are decreasing in α_A^1, and eventually firm A's profits are below those in the no information equilibrium.

The direct implication of this analysis is that firm A may not have an incentive to disclose targeted information, even if the generation and dissemination of that information is costless. This contrasts with symmetric targeted information, which always increases revenue. While targeted information can be both socially and privately productive, previous literature has shown that the incentive to gather and disseminate this information may be excessive from a social perspective. The next section reexamines this result for asymmetric information.

------

[15]Of course, if the targeted group is sufficiently large, and the change induced by the information is sufficiently large, condition (6) is no longer satisfied, and firm A increases its profits by revealing the information, and then selling to group 1 only.

18

IV. Welfare Analysis

Revelation of matching information of the type discussed in sections II and III yields a social benefit. The benefit results from consumers making more appropriate choices between brands. However, the information may be costly for firm A to generate and disseminate, and hence the welfare effect of the information is less clear. In this section, I consider whether the social gain to the information necessarily exceeds its costs.

The reason that information may be privately optimal, while reducing welfare is that the benefit to the firm of releasing the information comes about through its impact on prices. Because price increases induce transfers from consumers to producers, private profitability does not insure social desirability.

In fact, both A&R and M&S find that there is an excess incentive to provide matching information. In the A&R model, consumers can, in lieu of actually searching, spend money to acquire information about which brand best matches their tastes. Alternatively, they can search (e.g., visit retailers), in which case they observe both brand characteristics and prices. A&R show that equilibrium prices are decreasing in the percentage of consumers who choose to visit retailers, because search increases price competition between rival sellers. Because the marginal consumer ignores the impact his decision to avoid search has on prices (and therefore ignores the resultant transfer) there is excess information gathering. In M&S, firms can inform consumers of the match between the consumer and the two brands, at a cost which is increasing in the number of informed consumers. Again, for the marginal consumer the firms choose to inform, the social benefit of the improved matching is less than the marginal cost of informing that consumer (because the firm receives transfers from inframarginal consumers).

The representation of information in the model presented here is somewhat different from representations in the previous literature. This paper follows M&S in assuming that firms, rather than individual consumers, make the decisions as to whether to acquire information (in contrast to A&R). Hence, the assumption here is that consumers cannot take any action to improve their estimates of α_A^k. One important feature (especially for welfare) of the analysis from sections II and III that differs from the earlier work is that the size of the informed group is assumed exogenous in this paper, and therefore cannot on the margin be affected by the firm's actions. Hence, in this model, the existence of the transfer does not necessarily imply excess production of information.

A useful way of examining the divergence between social and private values of information is to consider the external effect of information. The change in welfare from the information is $\Delta W = \Delta\Pi_A + \Delta\Pi_B + \Delta CS$, where $\Delta\Pi_i$ is the change in firm i's profit, and ΔCS in the change in consumer surplus. If the external effect of the information, $\Delta\Pi_B + \Delta CS$, is positive, then information that is profitable for A to gather and disseminate is necessarily welfare enhancing. Hence, if $\Delta\Pi_B + \Delta CS$ is positive, then we can say that A has too little incentive to gather and disseminate information. Conversely, if $\Delta\Pi_B + \Delta CS$ is negative, then A has too much incentive. The following example indicates that, even in the symmetric case, there can be too little, or too much information generated.

Example 1: As in section III, let $f(R) = 1 + R$ for $R < 0$ and $1 - R$ for $R > 0$, where the support of $F(R)$ is $(-1,1)$. Consider symmetric drastic information such that all consumers are served. Because the information is symmetric, $\alpha_A^2 - \dot{\alpha}$ is also drastic, and the external welfare effect can be written

20

	Change in Consumer Surplus	Change in Firm B's Profits
Group 1	$\int_{-1}^{0} ((\alpha_A^1 - \hat{\alpha} + R)(1+R))dR - \Delta P$ $= .5(\alpha_A^1 - \hat{\alpha} - 1) + 1/3 - \Delta P$	-1/4
Group 2	$.5(\alpha_A^1 - \hat{\alpha} - 1) + 1/3 - \Delta P$	$1/4 + \Delta P$
Other Groups	$-\Delta P$	$\Delta P/2$

Summed over all groups, the external change in welfare is $2w_1 [(\alpha_A^1 - \hat{\alpha} - 1)/2 + 1/3] - \Delta P/2$. If $\alpha_A^1 - \hat{\alpha} = 1$, then $\Delta P = w_1/(1 - 2 w_1)$, and the external change is simply $2 w_1/3 - w_1/(2(1 - 2 w_1))$. This is positive for small w_1 (less than .125), and negative for large w_1 (> .125). Finally, since this expression is increasing in $\alpha_A^1 - \hat{\alpha}$, it follows that information which changes expectations dramatically is most likely to be underproduced. ∎

This example shows that, even in the symmetric case, firm A may have too little, or too much incentive to gather and disseminate information. If indeed the incentive to gather and disseminate information is excessive, it means that the information may in *total* have negative social value, which is a stronger result than in A&R and M&S (where production of information is only excessive on the *margin*).

One additional aspect of group size is worth noting. Information induces a transfer not only from consumers to producers, but also between consumers. Those consumers fortunate enough to be members of a group for whom α_A^k changes may become better matched to brands by virtue of the information, and experience increases in their welfare. In contrast, any consumer in a group with no informational change will be harmed by the information, due to a higher price. Since information about large groups is more likely to be profitable for firms to gather and disseminate (see Proposition

21

2), small groups are more likely to be adversely affected by information.

Finally, I consider the welfare effects of asymmetric information. Because there is no closed-form solution for prices in the asymmetric case, determining the external welfare effect of asymmetric information is more difficult than for symmetric information. Nevertheless, some observations can be made. First, as shown in section III, for non-drastic information A's price rises less for any α_A^1 when the information is asymmetric, rather than symmetric. Consequently, the transfer associated with any non-drastic α_A^1 is smaller, so that the external effect is larger in the asymmetric case (i.e., positive for a larger set of values for α_A^1 and w_1). In the drastic case, comparisons are more difficult. However, as Figure 5 demonstrates, some drastic information may actually reduce revenue, so that even if the cost of generating and disseminating it were zero, it would not be produced. In that case, there clearly is too little incentive for information generation. In general, it would appear that underproduction would be more of an issue for asymmetric information than for symmetric information. The following example helps illustrate this point.

Example 2 - Consider the specifications from Example 1, except here suppose the information is asymmetric. The external welfare effect of the asymmetric information is

	Change in Consumer Surplus	Change in Π_B
Group 1	$[\int_{-1}^{0} (\alpha_A^1 - \hat{\alpha} + R)(1 + R)dR] - \Delta P$ $= \dfrac{\alpha_A^1 - \hat{\alpha} - 1}{2} + \dfrac{1}{3} - \Delta P_A$	-1/4

Other groups	$$\int_{\alpha_A^k - \alpha_B + P_B - P_A}^{0} (\alpha_A^1 - \hat{\alpha} + R)(1+R)dR] -$$ $$\Delta P_A \int_{-1}^{\alpha_A^k - \alpha_B + P_B - P_A} (1+R)dR - \Delta P_B[\frac{1}{2} + \int_{\alpha_A^k - \alpha_B + P_B - P_A}^{0} (1+R)dR$$	$$\Delta P_B[\frac{1}{2} + \int_{\alpha_A^k - \alpha_B + P_B - P_A}^{0} (1+R)dR] +$$ $$\frac{\int_{\alpha_A^k - \alpha_B + P_B - P_A}^{0} (1+R)dR}{2}$$

To compare this expression to the symmetric case, suppose $\alpha_A^1 - \hat{\alpha} = 1$ and $w_1 = .25$. Then, $\alpha_A^k - \hat{\alpha} = -1/3$ for all other groups, and $P_A = .819$, $P_B = .92$. In that case, the external welfare effect is

$$\frac{\frac{1}{3} - \Delta P_A - \frac{1}{4}}{4} +$$

$$\frac{3[(\frac{1}{3} + P_A - P_B)(\frac{2}{3} - P_A + P_B + \frac{(\frac{1}{3} + P_A - P_B)^2}{3}) - \Delta P_A(P_B - \frac{1}{3} - P_A + \frac{(P_B - \frac{1}{3} - P_A)^2}{2} + \frac{1}{2}) + .5(\frac{1}{3} + P_A - P_B - \frac{(\frac{1}{3} + P_A - P_B)^2}{2})]}{4}$$

$= -.236/4 + 3(.191)/4 = .336$. Since the external effect was negative for these parameter values in the symmetric case, this suggests that asymmetric information is more likely to have positive external effects than symmetric information.

V. Discussion

The analysis in sections II and III assumes that the average quality of a brand is unaffected by the release of the targeted information. Hence, the news that a brand is particularly suited to a specific group is assumed to mean that it is less suitable for other groups. This interpretation is consistent with the analysis in A&R and M&S, and seems appropriate in some cases. For example, for pharmaceuticals, a drug's success rate in the overall population is established in the initial clinical trials, so that a rational consumer should interpret an increase in the success rate of the drug for a group to which she does not belong as a decrease in the likelihood the drug will work for her.

An alternative interpretation of targeted information is the news that a product is more appropriate for the targeted group has no effect on the perceived value of that product to the remaining population. In this case, the targeted information has two effects on consumers. It increases the average quality of the product, while simultaneously increasing the extent of differences across groups in the market. This latter effect was dealt with in sections II and III, while the effects of increases in one firm's quality are well-established (see, e.g., Tirole, 1988 at 296/7). Hence, the implications of this alternative interpretation of targeted information on prices and outputs can be readily discerned using the intuition from these other models.

In particular, the effects on prices of firm A's targeted information depend on whether the information is drastic. Drastic information shifts A's reaction curve out, while it leaves B's unchanged (its first-order condition is simply multiplied by (1-w), leaving its optimal price unaffected). Hence, drastic information leads to higher prices for both firms. In contrast, non-drastic information leaves the demand for brand B from non-targeted groups unchanged, while reducing the targeted group's demand for it. Hence, non-drastic information shifts B's reaction curve in, while shifting A's out, so that the net effect on both prices is ambiguous. However, under the F(R) analyzed in sections III and IV, this information causes B's price to fall while A's rises.

While the model assumes that consumers know their own ϵ_{ij}, I do not model how they learn their ϵ_{ij}'s. The model most readily lends itself to products which are "search" rather than "experience" goods, as the model is not dynamic. Vaccines would constitute an ideal example of such a product. In this case, an individual's ϵ_{ij} could be based on the side effect profile detailed in the (FDA-mandated) product inserts, e.g. the disutility a consumer places on nausea. If the good is an "experience" good, then ϵ_{ij} could represent past experience with the brand. For example, the ϵ_{ij} could reflect a patient's previous history with antibiotics for sinus infections   When a large percentage of patients have a significant history with the category of products, it is likely that the variation in individual tastes within a group would be large compared to differences across groups, so that $\bar{e}$ would be large compared to $\alpha_A^L - \hat{\alpha}$ (i.e., information will tend to be non-drastic).

VI. Conclusion

This paper explored the consequences of increasing the accuracy of information about product characteristics. Specifically, revealing information about the suitability of a brand for specific groups within the population induces better matching of consumers to brands. However, because better matching may induce price increases, the information may not improve either consumer or social welfare.

The goal of this paper was to examine how three features of the information can influence the price and welfare consequences of its release. Of particular interest I find that the size of the group to which the information pertains is an important determinant of its price effect. Holding the information content of the message fixed (how much it changes expectations), the price effect of the information increases more than proportionately with the size of the group. Hence, information that pertains to a large group is most likely to be profitable to disseminate. This provides two related reasons why it is disadvantageous to be a member of a small group. First, information relevant to the small group is less likely to be profitable to the seller. Second, information which has no effect on a specific group's expectations about the brands typically makes members of that group worse off. Since information is less likely to be produced for small groups, this implies that the information that does get produced will tend to harm members of small groups.

A second relevant aspect of information is whether it is symmetric. Asymmetric information generally leads to smaller price effects than symmetric information. In fact, asymmetric information may actually lower prices and revenues relative to the no information equilibrium, whereas symmetric information always raises prices and revenues. This implies that firms may choose not to differentiate themselves, contrary to what is sometimes called (e.g., Tirole,1988 at 267)) the "Principle of Maximum Differentiation." Finally, the information content of a message is an important determinant of its welfare consequences. Even though prices are non-decreasing in the information content of the message, the welfare effects are increasing in the information content over some range.

While this paper focuses on differentiation through information revelation, the results can also apply to changes in objective characteristics. For example, suppose there are two important features of a bicycle component; durability and weight, and different groups within the population value these features differently (recreational riders vs. commuters vs. racers). Consider the combination of durability and weight at which the utility of the median user in the population is maximized, subject to the production function. Suppose that firm A's rival has chosen this combination of durability and weight, and that firm A can (at some cost) produce a slightly different product (e.g., lighter, but less durable). This alternative product offers the same utility as the rival's product to most consumers in the population, but offers more utility to some groups, and less utility to others. For the reasons discussed in this paper, such a change might be profitable because it can increase the firm's profit-maximizing price. Moreover, one can use the analysis in this paper to show that the profitability of the change will be a function of the size of the group to whom this variety appeals. That is, producing the variety preferred by a sub-population will be more profitable if the sub-population is large, even if the additional total costs are proportional to group size.

References

Anderson, Simon and Regis Renault (2000) "Consumer Information and Firm Pricing: Negative Externalities from Improved Information" *International Economic Review*, 41, pp. 721-42.

Grossman, Gene and Carl Shapiro (1984)"Informative Advertising and Differentiated Products" *Review of Economic Studies*, 51, pp. 63-81.

Meurer, Michael and Dale Stahl (1994) "Informative Advertising and Product Match" *International Journal of Industrial Organization*, 12, pp. 1-19.

Reinganum, Jennifer (1988) `The Timing of Innovation: Research, Development and Diffusion' in Richard Schmalensee and Robert Willig (eds) *The Handbook of Industrial Organization.* Elsevier, Amsterdam, pp. 850-908.

Tirole, Jean (1988) *The Theory of Industrial Organization* MIT Press, Cambridge, MA.

Welch, Finis (1979) "Effects of Cohort Size on Earnings: The Baby Boom Babies' Financial Bust" *Journal of Political Economy*, 87, S65-98.

Figure 1 - Symmetric Equilibrium Price as a Function of $\alpha_1 - \hat{\alpha}$

for w = .1, e_{ij} uniformly distributed on (0,1)

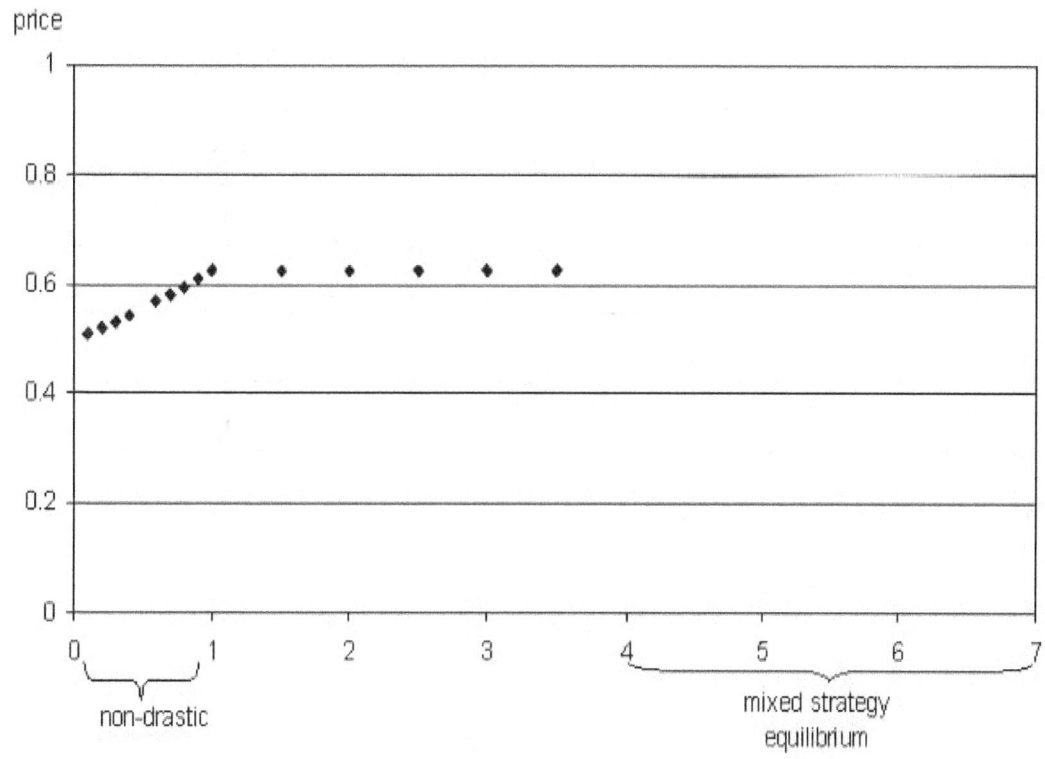

Figure 2 - P_A as a function of w_1 in symmetric and asymmetric equilibria
($\alpha_1 - \hat{\alpha}$ = .5)

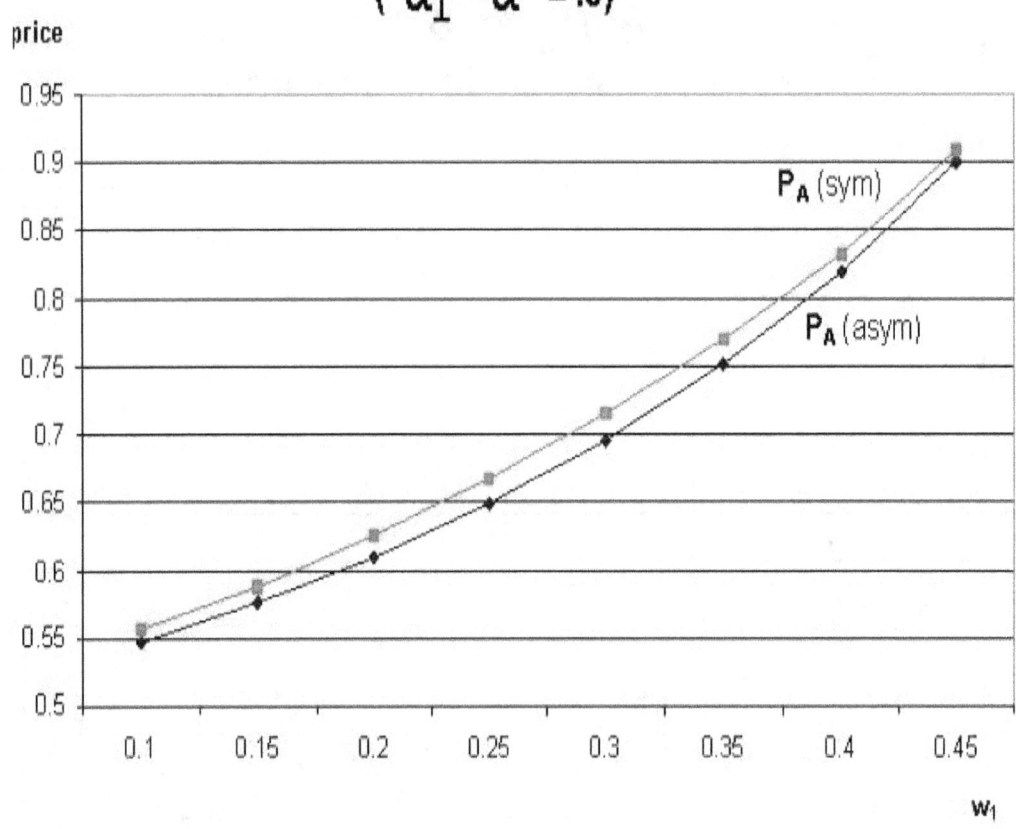

Figure 3 - Firm A's profits as a function of w_1
in symmetric and asymmetric equilibria

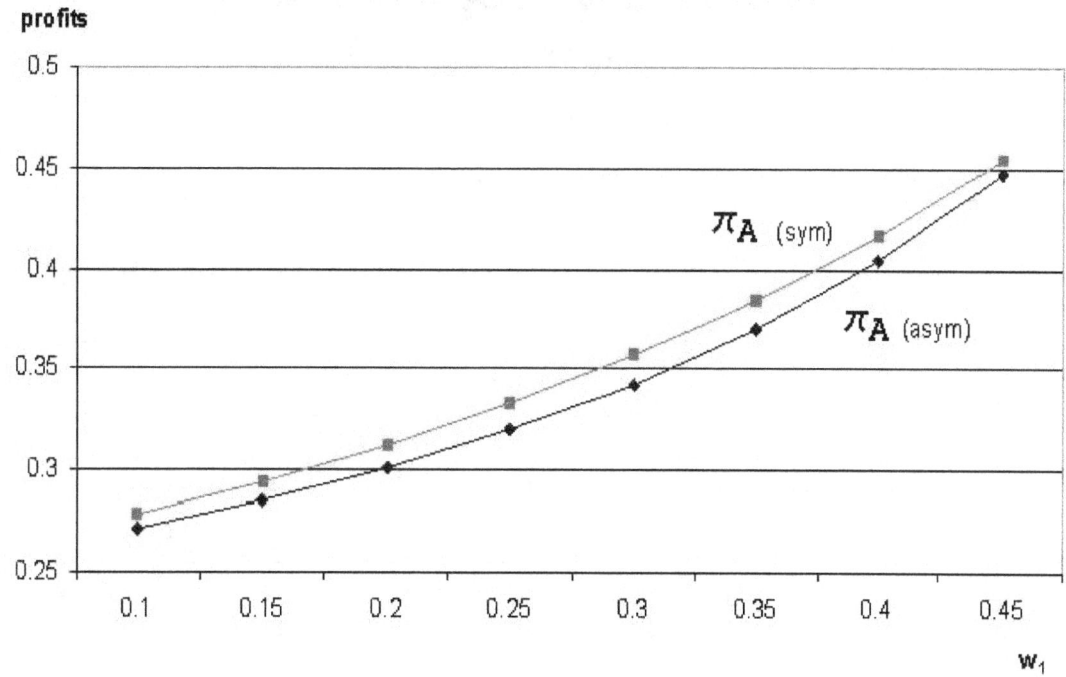

profits

π_A (sym)

π_A (asym)

w_1

Figure 4 - Firm A's Profits and Prices in the Asymmetric Equilibria as a Function of
$$\alpha_1 - \hat{\alpha}$$
for w = .25

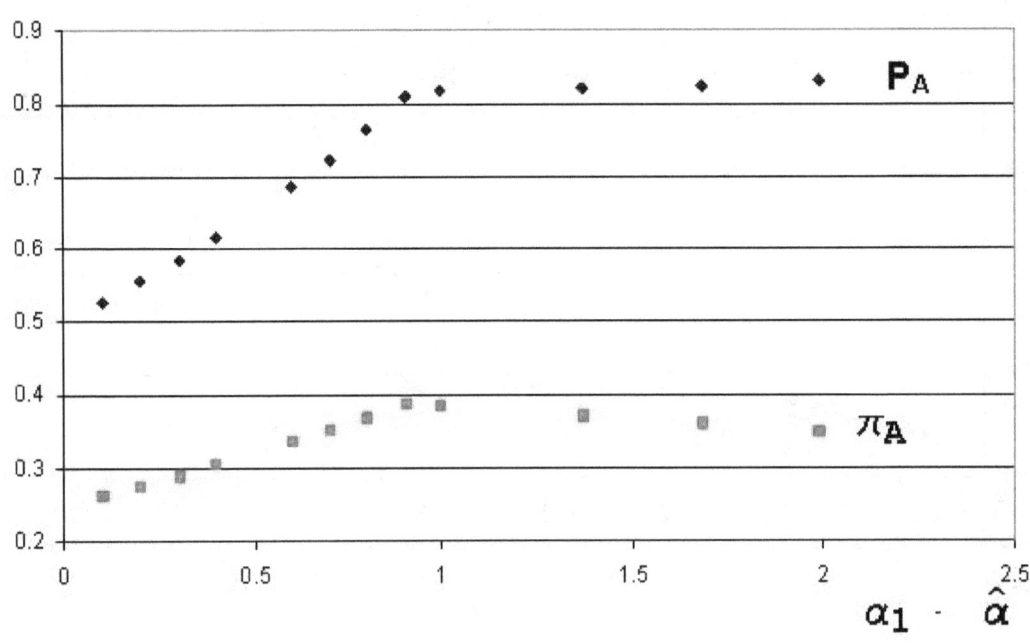

Figure 5 - Firm A's Prices and Profits in Asymmetric Equilibrium as a Function of $\alpha_1 - \hat{\alpha}$ (for $w_1 = .1$)

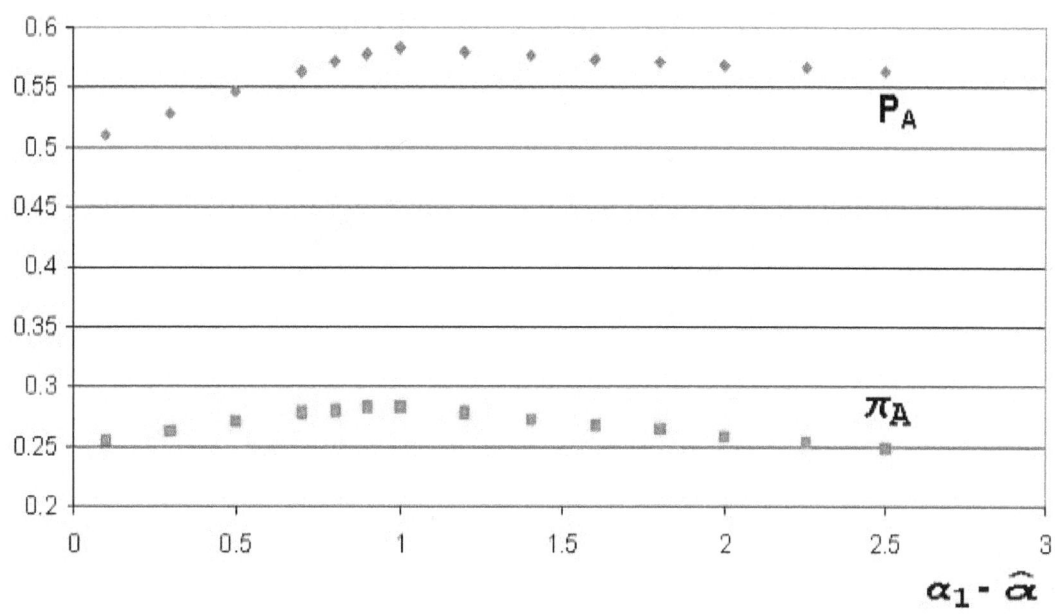

www.ingramcontent.com/pod-product-compliance
Lightning Source LLC
Chambersburg PA
CBHW081245170526
45165CB00009B/3204